The Town
Cemeteries and Gravestones
of Hadley, Massachusetts

HADLEY HISTORICAL COMMISSION

The Town Cemeteries and Gravestones
of Hadley, Massachusetts

WHITE RIVER PRESS
Amherst, Massachusetts

Town Cemeteries and Gravestones of Hadley, Massachusetts

Hadley Historical Commission

© 2009 Hadley Historical Commission. All rights reserved.

No portion of this book may be reproduced or used in any form, or by any means, without prior written permission of the publisher.

A PUBLICATION OF HADLEY'S 350TH CELEBRATION

White River Press
P.O. Box 3561
Amherst, MA 01004
www.whiteriverpress.com

Printed in the United States of America

ISBN: 978-1-935052-24-1

Front cover art based on photograph taken by Bob Drinkwater
Layout and cover design by Patricia Nobre

Library of Congress Cataloging-in-Publication Data:
The town cemeteries and gravestones of Hadley, Massachusetts / Hadley Historical Commission.
   p. cm.
Published in conjunction with the Hadley 350th Committee.
Includes bibliographical references.
ISBN 978-1-935052-24-1
1. Cemeteries--Massachusetts--Hadley--History. 2. Sepulchral monuments--Massachusetts--Hadley--History. 3. Hadley (Mass.)--Buildings, structures, etc. 4. Hadley (Mass.)--History. 5. Hadley (Mass.)--Genealogy. 6. Registers of births, etc.--Massachusetts--Hadley. 7. Hadley (Mass.)--Biography. I. Hadley Historical Commission (Hadley, Mass.) II. Hadley 350th Committee (Hadley, Mass.)

F74.H1T69 2009
929'.5--dc22
                              2010001927

Contents

Preface — i

I. Hadley's Town Cemeteries — 1
Hadley Historical Commission with Kayla Haveles

II. Carvers in the Old Hadley Cemetery — 39
by Bob Drinkwater

III. Highlights from Hadley's Town Cemeteries — 47
Fred Oakley with Laura Miller

Endnotes — 87

Preface

This volume dedicated to the history of Hadley's five town cemeteries presents information gathered by the Hadley Historical Commission in celebration of the town's 350th. Hadley cemeteries were included when the town first set out to document its historic resources in the 1980s, but the fairly cursory responses in the nomination to the state's Register of Historic Places made little reference to the history of gravestone art in Hadley, the changing nature of cemetery landscapes, or the history of the management and use of the cemeteries over time, so the Commission engaged the help of Kayla Haveles, a graduate student in the University of Massachusetts Amherst's Public History program, to comb town records and other sources in order to create a much richer portrait of that history. Her research on the five town cemeteries is synthesized here into a single essay that provides an overview of that story.

In addition to the benefits of our relationships with UMass, Hadley is fortunate to enjoy proximity to the Association for Gravestone Studies, headquartered in nearby Greenfield. Commissioners knew that Bob Drinkwater, a past president of the AGS, had compiled a good deal of research on the carvers whose work is present in Hadley's oldest burying ground. We invited Bob to publish an essay drawn from that work in this volume, and are delighted to share this fascinating information with interested readers.

Another active AGS member, Fred Oakley, has been a leader in cemetery conservation, in Hadley and well beyond. Fred's tours of the burying grounds have become enormously popular, and so we asked Laura Miller, another Public History student, to conduct a walking oral history with Fred, to capture some of his thoughts and insights about the stones he has so lovingly cared for over the years. This volume joins other recent tributes to Fred Oakley, whom we thank for his unwavering dedication to Hadley's cemetery landscapes. We also wish to thank Fred, as chair of the Cemetery Commission, for his help in the creation of this book.

The Commission also wishes to thank Rick and Mary Thayer and also Bob Drinkwater for their numerous contributions to this volume, including the lovely photography.

As you read these pages, we hope you enjoy learning about the generations past and how the choices they made about the town's cemeteries and the markers in them reflect larger developments in the history of Hadley. And we hope you notice, too, how much the survival of these special places has depended on the support of the town, formally through the allocation of funds for maintenance and also informally, through the contributions of men and women who have volunteered time and care to make sure these unique landscapes endure for the future. We hope that our counterparts at the 400th, and even 450th, anniversaries of the town's founding will have reason to look back on our era of stewardship with approval and gratitude.

The Hadley Historical Commission

Hadley's Town Cemeteries

Hadley Historical Commission with Kayla Haveles

"It is in burying grounds—in little villages of the dead—that artifacts bring us closest to the lives of the Connecticut Valley's former residents. Gravestones are the most numerous and evocative artifacts found in the towns lying along the Connecticut River. They number in the thousands. Yet each marker tells its own unique story of untimely death, forgotten ambition, filial piety, or lost love."[1]

Graveyards in Hadley from Settlement to the Civil War

Known in its earliest years as simply "the burying yard" and then as "Center Cemetery," Hadley's first burying ground was established in 1660 in what was then known as the Great Meadow. Created soon after the 1659 founding of the town itself, this cemetery served as the only burying yard for over a century and is the resting place of many of Hadley's founders.

Figure 1: Modern day view of the first town cemetery

As in towns across Massachusetts, the graveyard in those earliest years of settlement were "'literally boneyards, simply a place of burial and often located on infertile or leftover land considered undesirable for other uses"; the graveyard "reflected the general austerity and difficulty of life during this period and were intentionally unwelcoming as Puritans wanted as little as possible to do with the place of the dead."[2]

The men and women who settled Hadley believed that the physical remains of loved ones were nothing to dwell on: only the fortunes of the soul mattered. As part of their radical reforms of the Church of England—still tainted, they believed, by traces of Catholicism—Puritan migrants hoped to do away with role of clergy in funerals, sermons delivered over the body, and funeral processions. Concerned that churchyard burials promoted unwelcome fixation on ancestors, they chose a site for the burying ground that was well away from the meetinghouse on the Town Common, so that there would be no hint that the ground was considered in any way sacred.

Figure 2: Gravestone of Reverend Russell

Figure 3: Gravestone of Samuel Barnard and his daughter Hannah

Not all graves in these burying yards would have been marked, as only a few families were able to afford expensive stone markers. The oldest extant grave marker in the burying ground today is the 1688 stone for Rebekah Russell; inscribed in sandstone, a popular material at the time, are the words "Rebekah, made by God a meit help to Mr John Russell, and fellow labourer in Christ's work; a wise, vertuous, pious mother in Israel lyes here, in full assurance of a joyful resurrection. She died in the 57 year of her age, November 21, 1688." [for photos, see Part III][3] Table stones were reserved for clerical and civil leaders and their wives. The inscription on the stone of Reverend Russell is unusual in that it follows the four edges of the stone: "REVEREND RUSSELL REMAINS WHO FIRST GATHERED AND FOR 33 YEARS FAITHFULLY GOVERNED THE FLOCK OF CHRIST IN HADLY TIL THE CHEIF SHEPHERD SUDDENLY BUT MERCIFULLY CALLED HIM OFF TO RECEIVE HIS REWARD IN THE 66 YEAR OF HIS AGE DECEMBER 10 1692." Other table stones in Hadley mark the graves of Samuel Barnard and his daughter Hannah, whose cupboard became the subject of scholarly interest in the 1990s.[4]

Apart from these exceptions, the earliest stones in Hadley's oldest graveyards, in keeping with Puritan belief (and possibly a result too of an absence of trained and talented stonecarvers), have neither representational nor ornamental carving. In time, the need for religious radicalism waned and policies relaxed.

Winged death's heads "embodied the triumph of death and proclaimed the mortality of the flesh while simultaneously holding out the promise of the soul's triumph over death through a gracious rebirth."[5] As attitudes softened, the severe death's heads that ornamented the few graves that received stones began to look more and more like cherubs.[6]

As the eighteenth century wore on, the effects of the Great Awakening—an emotion-filled religious revival that rocked Britain's Atlantic colonies from the 1720s to the 1740s—came

Figure 4: Gravestone of Eunice Cook

Figure 5: Gravestone of Moses and Elizabeth Porter
Note the dual portraits of the deceased, a rare feature.

to be seen on headstones as emphasis shifted away from dour imaginings of the decaying body and toward more optimistic visions of eternal life. By the 1760s, visions of the afterlife as a time of judgment were supplanted by the hope of salvation. "Earths highest station ends in 'here he lies'/ But life immortal waits beyond the grave" reads the inscription of the 1755 marker for Moses Porter, who died while serving in the Seven Years War. With messages like this, burying grounds took on a more uplifting cast.

Figure 6: Gravestone of Horace Judd

Around this time, the preservation of the town's historic gravestones emerged as a concern. In one of the earliest extant records regarding the maintenance of Hadley's burying yard the town voted (7 March 1768) to repair the tombs and monuments over the graves of Reverend Russell and his wife, the first of many ways residents would pay homage to the town's founders and indicate an interest in preserving its historic markers.

In the decades following the American Revolution, gravestones again reflected changing times. Cherubs and angels gave way to other iconography that no longer drew attention on the body interred, but rather on the opportunity to contemplate loved ones in more abstract ways. Stones became less marker and more memorial. Urns and willows became common motifs (1810 Charles Lyman, Hockanum; 1832 Eunice Cook and 1831 Horace Judd, Center Cemetery). The willow (weeping willows being fashionable symbols of mourning) and urn (a motif popular in the neoclassical styles fashionable in the time, and

Figure 7: Gravestone of John Smith

also suggesting the containment of ashes) adopted at the turn of the nineteenth century had been the first glimmerings of a softening of attitudes toward death. In Center Cemetery, the urn and swag on the marker for John Smith (who died in 1818) is an especially nice example from this era.

As stones became increasingly associated with the mourning of individual lives, and less opportunities to remind the living to attend to the state of their souls, a rising number of stones include biographical text celebrating the person interred. Particularly

Figure 8: Gravestone of Chester Smith

poignant is the grave of Chester Smith, "instantly killed by the upsetting of a loaf of wood," killing the boy of eighteen (Center Cemetery).

Toward the end of the eighteenth century, the general preference for ordered landscapes began to reshape cemetery landscapes as well. Though cemeteries remained "rough and unadorned," with no ornamental planting or intentional landscaping, greater care was taken to align headstones, and fieldstone walls and wooden fences began to appear.[7]

While the markers present in Hadley's first cemetery reflected wider changes in the culture, a proliferation of new burial grounds reflected changes in Hadley as a town. Over time, settlement in Hadley expanded in every direction not bounded by the Connecticut River, as families moved beyond the Common and the meadows surrounding it. The area that is now known as Hockanum in the southern part of Hadley was settled by Captain John Lyman of Northampton, his son Zadok, and his daughter Mindwell Pomeroy and her husband Ebenezer. The

Figure 9: Plainville Cemetery today

area developed after the 1755 establishment of the Hockanum-Northampton ferry, and the country road laid out in 1761. Just a half-dozen years later, in 1767, the village established its own burial ground, making it the second oldest in town.

Settlement spread northward as well. Very early on, families had begun to settle in and around what is today Lake Warner. But until the end of the eighteenth century, most of the early inhabitants of North Hadley were probably buried in the so-called Center Cemetery. In 1790, the establishment of North Hadley Cemetery gave the area its own burial ground. Likewise, the neighborhood of Russellville had been settled about 1785 by Sunderland natives John and Daniel Russell and their brother-in-law, William Montague. They established large farms in the wooded area along the Connecticut River, and as the population of the village increased over the next several decades, the families established their own burial ground, too, in the second quarter of the nineteenth century. The area that is now known as Plainville in the eastern part of Hadley was settled by Josiah Nash and Samuel Gaylord, Jr. about 1790, and came to be known as Plainville in the early nineteenth century. The village established its own cemetery in 1802.

By the early nineteenth century, residents of Hadley had established burying grounds to serve five neighborhoods. Already, the town had looked to expand its original burial grounds at the village center, too. On 11 April 1791, townsmen voted to form a committee to survey and procure land to enlarge the Center burying yard, and land on the east side of the burial ground was secured.[8] A generation later, the town had once again outgrown the burying ground. In April 1827 another committee was charged with procuring land, either for a new burying yard or for another expansion of the existing one.[9] This committee reported (on 7 May) that it believed the town inhabitants preferred an expansion of the present burying yard, to the creation of a new one, and that good land for a new burying yard was not available in any case. It suggested that the town extend the present cemetery as far west "as the first path leading to the North so as to include an acre and half of additional land," which the owners of the land were willing to sell at a reasonable price. While the town initially voted to allow the same committee to buy, level, enclose, and lay out this extension, later in the meeting it reconsidered, and instead voted to send out a committee to survey the burying yard and report its opinion of the best place for an addition.[10] Within an hour the committee returned and reported that it unanimously agreed that the addition should be on the east side rather than the west. This new report was accepted and yet another committee was formed, to purchase, level, enclose, and lay out about two acres of land on the east side of the burying yard.[11]

In November 1828 the town voted to allow this latter committee to sell the lots by auction, provided that the committee selected and reserved lots for the use of the minister and his successors, for those inhabitants who could not afford a lot, and "for strangers, as they may think expedient."

Selectmen records also reflect the development of the management of the burying yard. Initially, there appears to have been little formal oversight. Despite an 1806 vote to appoint six wardens to superintend and regulate funerals, no town officials appear to have been charged with supervising the cemetery. In April 1825, however, the town voted that the Selectmen be authorized to appoint sextons for the several burying grounds in the town, suggesting the beginning of a more intentional approach to cemeteries.

The Victorian Era

For most of the nineteenth century, town records contain little comment about the cemeteries. Not until Hadley began to publish Annual Town Reports in the 1870s (a result of a new Massachusetts State Law requiring more uniform reporting) do regular statements appear. And at first, even those records are silent on the subject of cemeteries, since there are no Cemetery Committee reports until 1883. But other sources do shed some light on decisions that affected the cemeteries. Town expense reports in the 1870s, for instance, show large amounts of money spent on the care and repair of the cemeteries, particularly Center Cemetery and North Hadley Cemetery.

Continued population increases created an ongoing need to expand the various cemeteries. For instance, in order to augment the Plainville burial ground, in January 1886 land was bought from Smith Charities of Northampton. A new quarter board fence was erected around the entire cemetery, and local inhabitants helped to grade the land and cart in material to improve the soil.[12]

Figure 10: North Hadley's hills provided for a scenic landscape.

This improvement may also have been part of general Victorian era impulses to beautify cemeteries, as the Cemetery Committee reports continually comment on the improved appearance and care of the cemeteries throughout the 1870s, 80s, and 90s, both by the town and by private owners of lots. Across Hadley, as across Massachusetts and even the nation, Victorian-era interest in beautifying cemeteries transformed burial grounds. As early as the 1830s and 1840s, burying grounds around the Commonwealth began to reflect the influences of the "rural cemetery movement."[13] Inspired by cemeteries in New Haven and Paris around the turn of the nineteenth century, towns began to want more picturesque places to contemplate loved ones. In 1831, the Massachusetts Horticultural Society established Mount Auburn Cemetery. That the term "burial ground" itself fell out of use in these decades, as people increasingly preferred the term "cemetery" (from the Latin, 'to sleep'), was meant to suggest the landscape's new role as a site of "consolation and inspiration." Victorian families "lavished family plots with embellishments as an outward recognition of their sorrow."[14]

This increased interest in cemetery landscapes may have contributed to the establishment of Hadley's first formal Cemetery Committee in March 1861. Each cemetery was to have its own committee, whose members were "to retain office until others are chosen in their places…have power to establish drive ways, paths, lots, plant and remove trees, remove bodies and have the general supervision of the same." The chairman of the town meeting formed a committee of five to nominate a committee of three for each cemetery to carry out these provisions.[15]

In Hadley as elsewhere, the ever-changing national culture influenced cemeteries as well. New styles of gravestone art appeared. Family plots were edged with stone curbs (three excellent examples can be found in the North Hadley Cemetery, two for Smith families and another for the Grangers), or ringed with iron fences or shrubbery. In some cases a large central monument replaced individual grave markers. Obelisks (like the 1860 obelisk to mark the Bartlett family in Hockanum, or the memorial to John Smith and his wives in the Center Cemetery)

Figure 11: Bartlett family obelisk in Hockanum

reflected the passion for all things Egyptian that washed over Americans in the second quarter of the nineteenth century, prompted in part by Napoleon's adventures in Egypt at the close of the eighteenth century.

Artwork on stones, too, reflected evolving ideas about the afterlife, and new sentiments and preferences. Indicative of a certain softening is the shifting preference away from dark slate to white marble, and from severe rectangular slabs toward three-dimensional monuments. Though there is no statuary present in any of Hadley's cemeteries, smaller elements became more sentimental. Ivy cascades over the marker of Susan Phelps' 1875 stone in the North Hadley Cemetery, while a stone carrying the image of a piano marks an 1858 grave.

Figure 12: George Henry Clark grave (detail); The piano reflects Victorian preferences in cemetery art.

The landscape itself responded to these same influences. Varied topography and winding roads were now fashionable (as in architecture, the Victorians favored variety and asymmetry over simplicity and order), as were plantings that involved hedges, privacy screens or otherwise created a sense of enclosure. Hadley's cemeteries had all been well established before the rural cemetery movement unfolded, and, since so little documentation of Hadley's cemeteries in the mid-nineteenth-century survives, it is impossible to know when or to what degree Hadley residents embraced the new attitudes toward memorial landscapes. But many cemeteries tried to enhance their aesthetic value, and certainly by the last quarter of the nineteenth century, the first documented attention to the cemeteries as aesthetic landscapes began to appear. In 1877, 1894 and 1899, trees in the Center Cemetery were both consciously planted, and consciously removed.[16] From the late 1880s on mowing became a regular expense, as residents began to expect cemeteries to have a more managed appearance.

The middle decades of the nineteenth century also saw two new features in town cemeteries, both embraced in Hadley: a town tomb, and two hearse houses. The former—which Hadley built in 1859—was meant to hold bodies of the dead during months that the ground was frozen and graves could not be dug (with the advent of refrigeration, the town tomb fell into disuse). The building of hearse houses reflects a larger and more scattered population: as it became harder to carry the deceased from home to their burial spot, and increasing sentimentality and desire for ornament made plain wagons less than desirable, hearses and hearse houses became fashionable. As part of these efforts, in March 1861 the town voted to procure two hearses for the town, one for the north part of town and one for the central and southern parts. Later that year, the town voted to instruct the Selectmen to build two hearse houses at locations of their choosing. The hearse house at North Hadley was repaired and fence posts replaced in 1886; this may be the board-and-batten shed that still stands at the southwest corner of the cemetery.[17]

Figure 13: The 1859 "town tomb" in Center Cemetery

Another landscape feature—paths—also became more purposeful, whether they were straightened to be more orderly and functional, or made winding to be more aesthetically pleasing. The Selectmen's report for 9 February 1884 states that the town voted to "rebuild and straighten the Cemetery road in Great Meadow," which abutted the Center Cemetery. Work was undertaken to improve the entrance road to the North Hadley Cemetery in 1892. At some point "during the horse and buggy period," four roadways were laid out in the Plainville cemetery—perhaps the roadways were efforts to make the heretofore simple cemetery conform more closely to prevailing fashion as well.[18]

Fences also became increasingly important to cemetery landscapes. Town reports include increasing references to fencing in the last quarter of the nineteenth century. While, for instance, the townsmen voted to rebuild a fence around Hockanum Cemetery and raised some funds towards the

Figure 14: The cemetery in Russellville as it appears today

project in 1889, the February 1891 Cemetery Committee Report explains that it had not yet been erected because there was disagreement over what type of fence should be installed. Fences on the north, south, and west sides needed to be sufficiently strong to keep out animals from the adjacent fields, but "in the interests of good taste," the fence on the front had to be both strong and attractive. The following year the project was still delayed due to "difficulty in securing a portion of the necessary material," but it was finally completed in 1892. Though the type of fence selected is never mentioned, the expenses indicate that it involved at least in part wooden posts, and a historic photograph shows pickets.

Maintenance of fencing and grounds proved an ongoing concern in the coming decades. Although the 1895 Cemetery Committee Report notes that Hockanum residents had kept their cemetery in "respectable condition at their own expense," the committee was also responsible for repairing and painting the fence in 1896, 1905, and 1907. The town raised money in March 1889 to build a new fence around the Russellville cemetery.[19] It appears that Russellville was subsequently well-maintained, as the Cemetery Committee Report for 1896 notes the "excellent" appearance of Russellville; the fence was repainted in 1899 and again in 1905. The Cemetery Committee report for 1894 notes that the fences at Center Cemetery would soon need to be replaced, and the following year "a single rail placed upon the top of the stone posts" was suggested as a replacement fence on the front, west, and north sides.[20] In 1897, the committee replaced twenty-four 25-year-old decaying wooden hitching posts with iron ones, and cleared out more "wild growth," and in 1913 and 1914, an iron fence was finally erected on the south and east sides of the Center Cemetery (and a wire fence on the north and west sides), completed with an appropriation from the town.[21] Repairing and painting the fences, especially as they reached the half century mark in the late 1950s and early 1960s, was a constant expense during the remainder of the twentieth century.

The focus on these projects, however, left the Center Cemetery's most historic section in neglect. The 1919 Cemetery Committee Report noted the tidy appearance of the new section, but appeals to the descendents of those buried in the old section for more help and more funds to improve grading and fix broken headstones. Not only were funds a problem, but labor proved difficult as well. The Cemetery Committee report for the previous year lamented the "unusual difficulties" in caring for the cemeteries "owing to labor conditions," possibly a shortage due to the reorganization of the work force during World War I.

Among the most intriguing references in the committee reports from the Victorian era comes from 1892, when seats and a cover for a "Pavilion" were bought and installed at the Center Cemetery. What this was and where it stood remains a mystery, but a pavilion would have been the town's most significant effort to convert the original Puritan burying ground to a fashionable rural cemetery.

Also in 1892, a separate cemetery association was formed in North Hadley to "assist in the care and beautifying of their grounds."[22] The association's first major project, in conjunction with the town Cemetery Committee and with the help of a private financial gift, took place in 1895. The group graded, fertilized, and seeded certain sections of the cemetery, put headstones in line, removed footstones, and marked lots on a plan of the grounds with the family names of the plots.[23] The next year the efforts continued, this time through the town Cemetery Committee, by repairing and painting the hearse, and repairing the pump and canvass. The hearse house was painted the following year, and North Hadley was used as an example to the other cemeteries due to its equal grading of plots, which "gives it a much more agreeable effect, and it also lessens the labor and expense of care."[24] The efforts of both the North Hadley Association and the town Cemetery Committee helped this landscape to conform to prevailing ideas about cemetery beautification.

Population changes

Over the course of the nineteenth century, two large waves of immigration—first from Ireland and then from Poland—brought new communities of Catholic residents to Hadley. They worshiped in a number of churches in Hadley and Amherst, and established a Catholic cemetery in 1870, when the St. Bridget's cemetery at Plainville in Hadley was consecrated by Archbishop Williams. In 1926, a second cemetery, associated with Hadley's Holy Rosary Parish, was established; a small chapel (which also served as a tomb in the winter months) was built there in 1929.[25] As a result of the development of these two cemeteries for the Catholic community, large numbers of Hadley residents would be buried there, rather than the five town cemeteries, a development that shaped the nature of the memorial art present and absent in the Hadley town cemeteries, as well as their rate of development, since the pressure on the land present from the founding eased in the middle to late decades of the nineteenth century and early decades of the twentieth.

The Twentieth Century Begins

Cemetery Committee reports in the nineteenth and twentieth centuries make plain the importance of volunteer leadership in the care of the cemeteries. Franklin Bonney—the chairman of the Cemetery Committee since at least 1883 when the earliest extant published reports begin—had served on the committee since its formation in 1861 and did not retire from the post until 1900. After forty years of service, Bonney's 1900 withdrawal from the Cemetery Committee resulted in some lapsing of efforts on the behalf of the town's cemeteries. The Cemetery Committee does not appear in the Annual Town Reports from 1900 to 1905, and in February 1906 the town voted to authorize the Selectmen to appoint a new committee to take charge of Center Cemetery. This reorganization spurred a new round of improvements, as it was also voted to appropriate funds to grade and improve the cemetery the coming year. But new leadership was needed. In the reports for both 1919 and 1922, special thanks are given to Franklin's son, Charles W. Bonney, for his help in maintaining the cemeteries. Bonney would himself have another long tenure as caretaker.

As Hadley entered a new century, the town once again looked to improve and expand its main burial grounds. In 1907, $50 was paid to William C. Dickinson for a half acre of land; according to the deed, the land entrusted to the Cemetery Committee was situated in the Great Meadow, bordered on the south by a meadow road, on the east by land of one Smith and one Coggewell, on the north by the Connecticut River, and on the west by other land of Lewis S. and William C. Dickinson, co-owners of the purchased land.[26] As there were no more vacant lots, the committee also suggested that one acre of land be purchased on the east side of the cemetery. This suggestion was carried through, and the town reports for 1908 indicate that $608.65 was paid for land and surveying. After the new addition was laid out, markers were ordered and installed to outline the new lots in 1911.[27]

While the formation of a new committee revitalized efforts towards maintaining the cemetery, there may also have been other forces at work. At various moments in the cemetery's history special attention was paid to its appearance, a case in point being the 250th anniversary of Hadley's settlement in 1909. The Quarter-Millennial Committee, formed to prepare festivities for the celebration, suggested that special care be taken to maintain the good condition of the cemeteries. Some hint of the significance Center Cemetery took on in the wake of this event can be seen in its renaming: at this time Hadley's first cemetery officially began to be perceived as a historic landscape. It is in the town report for the year ending 10 February 1912, that Center Cemetery is referred to for the first time as Old Hadley Cemetery, suggesting a change in how the cemetery was viewed by the citizens of the town. Some new memorials began to appear in which twentieth-century families honored their seventeenth-century ancestors—for instance, in 1910, descendents of Peter Tilton erected a memorial stone in Old Hadley Cemetery.

At the same time that the cemetery was taking on new meaning as a historic place, it also became a site of early twentieth-century patriotism. For instance, one of the earliest acts of Hadley's

Figure 15: Peter Tilton stone in Old Hadley Cemetery

Daughters of the American Revolution chapter was marking the graves of Hadley's Revolutionary War soldiers. Hadley like many towns began to hold Memorial Day ceremonies at the town's cemeteries, a tradition the town continues to carry on today.

Another outgrowth of this increased interest in cemeteries may be the Russellville Cemetery Association, incorporated in 1911 "for the purpose of managing, caring for, improving and embellishing the burial ground set apart and known as the Russellville cemetery." Formalizing an existing, but unincorporated, Association, this new entity would administer funds "for the care, maintenance, protection, improvement or enlargement of its cemetery, or any lot, monument, fence or structure therein, or for planting and cultivating trees, shrubs or plants, or otherwise improving the premises in a manner consistent with the objects of the corporation."[28]

By the end of the first decade of the twentieth century, the Cemetery Committee began to stress the need for continuous funds in order to keep the cemeteries in good and orderly condition. A new approach was implemented: Perpetual Care (today, many stones marked "Perpetual Care" can be found throughout the cemeteries). While the money earned from the sale of lots in the new section of Old Hadley Cemetery was an important source of income, Perpetual Care Funds also became a significant means of support for the Cemetery Committee. The town report for 1909 notes that 60 lots were cared for by individual subscription over the previous year, and two lots were cared for out of trust funds set up for the purpose of perpetual care. The 1910 report encouraged citizens to establish Perpetual Care Funds, and included a circular the committee was to have printed for the purpose of persuading more plot owners to do so.

Figures 16, 17, and 18: Markers placed by the Daughters of the American Revolution, the Sons of the American Revolution, and the Perpetual Care funds

In 1922, the Cemetery Committee began to establish Perpetual Care Funds for each cemetery. Plainville Cemetery established its first Perpetual Fund in that year; there were several new funds established for Plainville in 1923, and then one every few years thereafter. In 1922 North Hadley Cemetery also created its first Perpetual Fund; however, the North

Hadley Cemetery Association retained control of that cemetery's funds. The first Perpetual Fund for Russellville was recorded in the Cemetery Committee Report for 1932.

A turning point in the management of the town's cemeteries came in 1927, when the Cemetery Committee was reorganized after the retirement of the caretaker of Old Hadley Cemetery, Charles Bonney. Each of the five town cemeteries received its own representative in the committee. The Town Warrant of December 31, 1927 outlined the new structure:

> Article 30. To see if the town will vote to authorize the Selectmen to appoint a Cemetery Committee of five (5) members, one each to represent Old Hadley Cemetery, North Hadley Cemetery, Russellville Cemetery, Plainville Cemetery and Hockanum Cemetery, each for a term of three years and to further empower them to fill any vacancies that may occur on said committee from time to time for the unexpired term. Said Committee shall have full charge of the care of the town cemeteries. They shall organize by electing one of their number as Chairman and three members as an Executive Committee to direct the care of the cemeteries and purchase supplies for the use of the Caretakers and approve purchases for cemeteries and present them to the town for payment subject to the limits of the appropriation for the purpose. Said Committee to make an annual report to the town of their doings.

While this structure would not be stringently followed every year, the intent was to make the committee more organized, efficient, and productive.

The 1930s

It was not long before the newly-constituted committee would find itself challenged considerably as crises both fiscal and meteorological beset the town. During the Great Depression, the diminished returns of the perpetual funds caused a serious problem for the Cemetery Committee.[29] Trouble financing cemetery maintenance would be a recurrent theme throughout the twentieth century, reaching a fever pitch in the 1930s and early 1940s.

At the same time, interest in the cemeteries had never been greater. Though the New England Historic Genealogical Society had been founded in Boston in 1845, and the late nineteenth and early twentieth century saw the emergence of organizations focused on lineage, like the Daughters of the American Revolution and the Society of Mayflower Descendents, genealogy did not become a widespread popular hobby until the twentieth century. The National Genealogical Society was founded in 1915 (offering the *The National Genealogical Society Quarterly*), and the *Magazine of American Genealogy* first appeared in 1929. The national trend came to Hadley in earnest in the early 1930s. The town had so many visitors in the years 1932 and 1933 that not only did the Cemetery Committee Report for 1933 take note of the "hundreds of people from many states" visiting the town's burying grounds, but an article in *The Springfield Republican* on 1 January 1933 described the vast number of visitors—mostly women—from all over the country who came in search of their ancestors.[30] In 1934, Walter E. Corbin of nearby Florence transcribed inscriptions throughout the oldest sections of the Old Hadley Cemetery (available today in the Hadley Town Hall); four years later he completed a similar compilation for Hockanum.[31]

In addition to the large waves of visitors who came to find their ancestors in the cemetery in the 1930s, town inhabitants and outside benefactors paid increasing attention to the Old Hadley Cemetery. In 1932 alone, the Marsh family improved their large lot in the old section; Mr. Rockwell Smith and Mrs. Leslie R. Smith donated a large number of Norway Spruce and cedar nursery stock to replace trees that had died in the new section; and two

Figure 19: Vegetation in the Old Hadley Cemetery today

monuments were erected in the old section to the first settlers–one for Nathaniel Dickinson (erected in November), and a large boulder and bronze tablet (erected in January) in honor of the John Taylor family.[32] The donations continued the following year, with gifts of twenty evergreen trees from Mrs. Florence Marsh of Washington, D.C., two Colorado Spruce from the Connecticut Dickinson Association of Hartford, Connecticut, and a shrub from an Ohio cemetery for the site of a new memorial to Hadley's first settlers from Mrs. Myrtie Willing of Phelps, New York.

Figure 20: Dickinson plaque in Old Hadley Cemetery

Figure 21: Taylor plaque in Old Hadley Cemetery

The rest of the decade would prove challenging, due not only to the Great Depression, but also to the hurricanes of 1936 and 1938, which flooded large parts of the town and cemetery. Federal aid from the Emergency Relief Administration (ERA) and the Works Progress Administration (WPA), however, would prove beneficial not only to the old section of Old Hadley Cemetery, but to every cemetery in town. As early as 1934, New Deal funds had first begun to make their way to Hadley, some of which provided for work in the cemeteries. In 1934 and 1935, ERA administrator and town selectman Seymour H. Parker secured a project to straighten stones and generally restore the older sections of the cemetery. Some thirty-eight truckloads of loam were acquired to undertake improvements to the grading.[33]

Although the Emergency Relief Administration projects focused on Old Hadley Cemetery in 1934, Hockanum received attention in 1935.[34] The front fence was removed, a new fence installed on the north side abutting the addition. A wall of trap rock and cement was erected across the front of the cemetery, along the road. The rock was a gift from Charles Lyman of South Hadley; it was dug out of the quarry by the ERA, and trucked by the town. Federal funds and local donations significantly reshaped the landscape at Hockanum. In addition, Russellville's wooden fence was repaired and painted white by the ERA in 1935, and that same year North Hadley's iron fence was painted with aluminum paint, also by the ERA.

Figure 22: Stone fence at Hockanum

Figure 23: Old Hadley Cemetery after the 1936 flood

This work would in many ways be repeated by the WPA after the devastating 1936 flood. Parts of the Old Hadley Cemetery were under as much as five feet of mud, hundreds of stones were uprooted or broken, and trees, logs, and even parts of a bridge were deposited among the stones.[35] A grant was awarded for the project based on the criteria that it involved "repairs to an Historical Monument of great value." The project included resetting and replacing stones, removing silt, resetting monuments and replacing the iron and wire fences. The Civilian Conservation Corp dug out the road to the cemetery and those within the cemetery, and a road project on nearby West Street took silt from the cemetery to use in their own work. The project was completed on 14 July 1936.

Just two years later, the September 1938 hurricane threatened to destroy the work done by the ERA and WPA once again. Seven large trees were uprooted and destroyed, stone and marble slabs were broken, fencing damaged, and the older section of the cemetery was covered with four feet of water. Compared to the devastation of the 1936 flood, however, the Cemetery Committee found the damage manageable, and the WPA removed the elms and stumps of the destroyed trees.[36] The WPA also helped Plainville to pull back and reset some cedars that had been damaged by the hurricane.

Toward the Present

Though these weather events of the 1930s are better remembered today, a hurricane in 1955 resulted in similar damage to the town's cemeteries. Several trees were killed by lightning and required removal, and about seventy-five graves caved in, leading the committee to adopt a policy to exclude wooden vaults in the future to prevent cave-ins.

No Cemetery Committee reports were submitted for the Annual Town Reports from 1943 to 1953, so there is little indication of what actions were taken during those years. Certainly World War II directed attention elsewhere, and it took some time for the cemeteries to regain attention. Eventually, however, there was another revitalization of effort on behalf of the cemeteries. In

1955 the Cemetery Committee instituted several new rules as an attempt to avoid some issues concerning the care of individual lots and the cemetery as a whole. The price of burial lots rose, and the town no longer sold lots without an agreement for perpetual care. In addition, the Committee required that new monuments and headstones be approved by the committee; burials could not be made until the lot was paid for, the deed obtained, and perpetual care arranged; and the planting of any new vegetation needed to be approved by a given cemetery's designated superintendent.[37] In 1956 the Cemetery Committee embarked on a six-year project to repair and paint the North Hadley fence, since it had not been painted for twenty years, since the 1935 ERA work.

From 1954 to 1956, the Cemetery Committee worked to improve additions to the Hockanum cemetery that had been made in recent years. Preparation work was begun in 1954, including extending the stone wall across the front of the cemetery and digging a foundation trench. The stone for the extension of the wall was again donated by Charles Lyman of South Hadley, from his farm quarry, and a 1948 donation from Roger Johnson intended for improvements to the addition provided funds for building expenses. In 1955 the stone wall was completed with more stones donated by both Charles and William Lyman, "whose ancestors started the cemetery, around Revolutionary times." Stuart Russell also provided the use of his tractor. Work on the addition was completed in 1956 with the division of the burial lots, marked by terra cotta tile pins.[38]

At mid-century, more treework was performed, and trees were trimmed or removed. A dying elm and an at-risk maple at North Hadley Cemetery were taken down during the 1956 and 1957 seasons.[39] The 1960s saw similar care at North Hadley: dead branches were trimmed, and a large elm removed when it threatened to damage cars. A rock maple that had been struck by lightning was taken down in 1965. Finally, the owners of plots at North Hadley became impatient with the use of a well, and through a combination of solicitation and Cemetery Committee funds town water was installed, three faucets dispersed throughout the cemetery, and the well filled in with gravel.[40]

As in the 1930s, Hadley cemeteries again became places of interest to many, locally and nationwide. The late 1950s and early 1960s saw another large wave of outside visitors to the cemeteries, particularly the older sections. The 1957 and 1958 Cemetery Committee Reports again comment on the large number of visitors, suggesting that the approach of the 1959 tercentenary had drawn increasing attention to the cemeteries. And indeed, the 1959 Cemetery Committee Report confirmed that the 300th anniversary brought many visitors to the cemeteries. The late 1960s also saw the rise of a new fad: grave rubbing. In 1962 a couple from the University of California working under a grant from a national foundation took great interest in the earlier sections of the cemeteries. They took grave rubbings of patterns on the stones between 1660 and 1817.[41] The 1967 report also mentions extensive grave rubbing, mostly of pre-1817 stones, by visitors who attended Expo 67, the 1967 World's Fair held in Montreal, and then traveled to Hadley, looking for ancestors. Visitors from Texas to Northern Michigan as well as students from the nearby colleges came to Hadley cemeteries to take rubbings. The practice is mentioned in almost every report from 1967 to 1971, discussing the problems with litter and parking caused by the increased visitation. As in previous times, renewed genealogical interest resulted in new attention to memorials and monuments. In 1965, for instance, Edward Marsh of Purceville, Virginia, donated funds to repair and reset stones in the oldest section of the cemetery, while the descendents of Timothy Nash, the head of a pioneer family who settled in Hadley in 1661, erected a granite memorial in 1968, also in the oldest section of the cemetery.[42]

Unfortunately, the same period, the late 1950s through the 1960s, also saw increasing vandalism. Slight damage was noted in the report for 1959, mostly littering and tipping stones. In 1964, however, vandalism, "apparently caused by young boys," resulted in the overturning of several monuments, two of which could be reset, but also others that had already been restored after the 1936 flood and could not be repaired again.[43] Vandalism appears to have been a persistent problem throughout the decade, for the report for 1971 writes that there was less vandalism than usual, though a "drinking party" in the winter resulted in several stones pushed over and beer cans left strewn about.

The early 1970s brought about a major change in management of the cemeteries with the retirement of Frank Reynolds. While two members of the Cemetery Committee—Frank Reynolds and Oscar Johnson—were noted in the 1970 report for serving for over fifty years, it appears to be the retirement of Reynolds in 1972 that most affected the maintenance of the cemeteries. The last major project under Reynolds was the removal of a large, old weeping willow in the Old Hadley Cemetery that was beginning to crowd lots. Just as after the retirement of Franklin Bonney in 1900, the cemetery committee after Reynolds' retirement underwent a period of decline. This time, however, the gap was much longer: no cemetery report appears in the Town Records for thirty years, from 1973 to 2003.

In these years, attention to the cemeteries came from other directions. The Hadley Historical Society formed in 1973, and incorporated in the year of the nation's bicentennial, 1976.[44] The Hadley Historical Commission was organized in 1974. The Hadley Center Historic District was successfully nominated to the National Register of Historic Places in 1977 (and in the mid 1980s a new initiative was launched to expand the boundaries of the earlier district to include some 2,500 acres and about 700 properties), naming the town's oldest cemetery as a significant resource of historic value to the town, state and nation.[45] As that nomination made its way through the review process, work was also undertaken to establish historic districts in Hockanum and North Hadley, which gave those cemeteries National Register recognition as well.

The lack of formal Cemetery Committee Reports in the last quarter of the twentieth century does not necessarily mean that no actions were taken on behalf of the cemeteries. During the 1990s, information on Old Hadley Cemetery can also be gleaned from reports filed by the Historical Commission, which stepped in to help oversee the cemeteries while the town's Cemetery Commission was inactive. The Historical Commission Report for 1994 writes that the commission had met with Fred Oakley, who had begun helping to maintain stones in the Old Hadley Cemetery. A 10 September 1995 newspaper article in the *Daily Hampshire Gazette* indicates that Oakley and Hadley's First Congregational Church had begun repairing stones, including the restoration of Deacon Joseph Eastman's stone (1760). The Historical Commission Report for 1999 outlines the completion of a tree-removal project in Old Hadley and North Hadley, undertaken with funds from the Massachusetts Department of Environmental Management's Historic Landscape Preservation Grant program. Trees at Old Hadley were "removed if damaged, pruned, and cabled as needed." The cemetery was also surveyed, resulting in the mapping of 748 gravestones, including photographs and recorded data, which were compiled into six volumes and placed in the Town Clerk's Office. Gravestones were also repaired, replaced, cleaned, and reset as needed, undergrowth was trimmed, and the east fence replaced.

As the twentieth century drew to a close, among the more interesting challenges that came before the Cemetery Commissioners was the advent of new styles of gravestone art. In the final decades the century, advances in technology transformed the options available to families choosing memorials to loved ones. The decades that had followed the close of the Victorian era saw a comparative conservatism in gravestone art; stones on the whole became plainer and more reserved. But by the 1990s, gravestones began to reflect an emerging cultural preference for individual expression and customization. Innovations in laser etching and the ability to transfer photographs to stone allowed stones to carry images of beloved pets, boats and motorcycles, and even images of the deceased, while solar-powered lights became popular gravestone accessories. Far from the pedantic reminders of mortality that marked 17th-century graveyards, stones became opportunities to memorialize loved ones almost as a museum exhibit might.

A unique cluster of stones in the Hockanum cemetery illustrates this phenomenon, and in fact predates it. The Johnsons were the first local family to initiate in Hadley what has now become a trend nationwide. Stones chosen by members of this family harken back to the past while also embracing these new preferences in gravestone art. Mimicking the styles of eighteenth-century stones, the headstone's rounded tympanum and the inscribed tablet beneath being bordered with decorative vine carving, the stones of Clifton Johnson (1865-1940) and his wife Anna Tweed McQuestion (1876-1954) are celebrations of their lives, accomplishments and unique personalities. Johnson's stone writes, "Author, Traveler, Historian, Editor and Illustrator, Farmer, Lover of Nature, Good and Generous Citizen, he has achieved success who has left this world better than he found it." The reverse of Johnson's stone lists the books he published, while the reverse of the stone for Anna McQuestion refers not only to the beloved grandmother's life, but also the unique monument erected to commemorate it, the "granite laughter, marble tears, which was about unusual gravestones like this."

Figure 24 and 25: The front and reverse of Anna Johnson's unusual stone

When Irving McClure Johnson (1905-1991) and Electa "Exy" Johnson (1909-2004) followed some years later, the stones erected to mark their graves celebrated their careers as sailors and authors. A stone for Roger Johnson (1901-1988) and Elsie Welts Johnson (1898-1978 includes a tribute to their landmark bookstore (1918-

Figure 26: Irving McClure Johnson grave (detail); another Johnson family memorial

1978), but also their antique bicycle collection and interest in spelunking [for image see p. 86]. The gravestone of Arthur Cook Johnson (1935-1988) is topped by the universal symbol for recycling.

The Twenty-first Century Begins

Finally in 1999, a new Town Cemetery Committee was formed and "charged with developing a maintenance plan for all cemeteries."[46] The Historical Commission worked with the new Cemetery Committee for the next few years, outlining the needs of the cemeteries. In 2002 "management and administrative issues" for the Cemetery Committee were resolved, and contracts for mowing and leaf removal were secured for each of the five cemeteries.[47] The revitalization of the Cemetery Committee sparked a new burst of activity to restore the cemeteries themselves. In 2002, Matthew Beynon of Belchertown documented part of North Hadley Cemetery for his Eagle Scout project. About 100 young people attending a national meeting of the Mormon Church at the

University of Massachusetts documented more than 202 stones, equaling about one third of the cemetery. The year 2003 saw the completion of a Gold Scout documentation project of Russellville Cemetery by Emma Dragon of North Hadley. The project included a database of each grave and monument's inscription and epitaph, which were keyed to its lot on a map.[48]

As Hadley entered the twenty-first century, the town once again prepared to celebrate its founding, now 350 years ago. The Cemetery Committee looked to make its own preparations for the celebration. The 2004 report addresses the 2009 anniversary in its plans, stating that the committee hopes to have all the town cemeteries completely documented by the anniversary year. This included entering inscriptions into a database, though transcription was difficult as of many of the stones were illegible due to erosion, unique lettering styles, and soiling of the stones.[49] Also in preparation for the 350th, the Cemetery Committee replaced the decayed fencing at Russellville.[50]

The leadership of Fred Oakley (also active in the Association for Gravestone Studies) resulted in extensive work to restore Old Hadley Cemetery. In 2001, the Hadley Historical Commission reported that Oakley, with the help of men from the Community Service Section of the Hampshire County Correctional Facility, reset or cast new bases for 88 "at risk" stones. In 2002, the commission reported Old Hadley's participation in the town's first Hadley History Day, by the inclusion of a guided tour of the cemetery led by Oakley.[51] He supervised three workshops held at Old Hadley in collaboration with Holyoke and Greenfield Community Colleges, which taught participants methods and materials for repairing gravestones, but which also repaired many stones in the process. He held five similar workshops in 2004 in cooperation with Greenfield Community College's Community Education Workshops, which resulted in the repairing of 27 stones in Old Hadley. Workshops repaired twenty stones in 2006, and the process was expected to continue the following year.[52]

Also in response to the approaching 350th anniversary, in 2005 the Cemetery Committee embarked on projects to improve each of the town cemeteries using Community Preservation Act funds and cemetery funds.[53] Tree and fence work were performed at Hockanum, North Hadley, Old Hadley, and Plainville. The need for tree work had been apparent since 1997, when strong winds knocked down a tree in Old Hadley Cemetery, damaging several seventeenth-century graves, including the 1688 table-stone monument of Rebekah Russell.[54] Now, several years later, the north and west boundary fences at Old Hadley were rusted and overgrown with invading vegetation, and several trees needed to be trimmed or removed. The committee once again enlisted help from the Hampshire County House of Correction to start the process by cutting and piling brush and saplings around the fence edges, and new post and rail fences were erected. The Plainville fences were also replaced and vegetation removed, as the wood picket fence was decayed and the wire perimeter fence was "encased with saplings and brush." An arbor vitae hedge had once been planted as a privacy screen, but it had been allowed to grow until it became problematic and now required removal. The cemetery took on an appearance much closer to its original form in the early nineteenth century.

The history of Hadley's cemeteries is complex, following the course of developments in society both locally and nationally. The Victorian desire to improve cemeteries, the push for restoration in the mid-twentieth century begun with the work of the ERA and WPA, and most recently the efforts of the Cemetery Committee, have all played a part in the most significant changes in the town's cemeteries. Likewise, thanks to the service of longtime superintendents, such as Franklin Bonney, Frank Reynolds, and Fred Oakley, combined with the help of the cemetery commissioners and many other volunteers, our cemeteries have remained important places for residents, as well as descendents of inhabitants throughout the country. But they need our continuing care: as of July 2009, gravestone conservator Fred Oakley estimates that approximately eighty stones in Hadley's town cemeteries need attention. As Kevin Sweeney has mused, each of those markers "tells its own unique story of untimely death, forgotten ambition, filial piety, or lost love," stories that together create the history of our community.[55]

Carvers in the Old Hadley Cemetery

Bob Drinkwater

In Hadley, as in most colonial New England towns, a burying ground was set aside soon after the first settlers arrived. It was located in the northwest corner of what we now know as Old Hadley Cemetery. Sylvester Judd (*The History of Hadley*) could find no record of a vote to establish the burying ground, but cited evidence that it was in use by 1661. John Webster (ancestor of Noah Webster), who died April 5, 1661, is thought to have been the first person buried there (though Judd notes that an unnamed infant may have been buried there earlier the same year). Over the years, the burying ground was expanded southward and eastward to its present limits, each expansion marking a stage in the transition from colonial burying ground to modern cemetery.

Hadley's place in the history of the Connecticut River Valley

As Judd noted, the oldest monuments are the tablestones for Rev. John Russell and his first wife, Rebekah, purchased by the administrator of Rev. Russell's estate in 1693. There are a few gravestones with earlier dates, but all are known or suspected to have been placed at a later time. For example, the stone for

Figure 27: Gravestone of John Webster

Dr. John Westcarre is known to have been purchased in 1737, sixty-two years after Westcarre died. And the marble stone for John Webster was erected by his descendants in 1818, one hundred and fifty-seven years after he died. As you walk about Old Hadley Cemetery, you may note several modern monuments commemorating Hadley's earliest settlers, many of whom previously lay in unmarked graves.

From the 1720s onward, the practice of marking graves and commemorating the deceased with gravestones became more commonplace. In Hadley, as in much of the lower Connecticut Valley, all but a few of the gravestones erected prior to 1780 are sandstone. Some, like the tablestones for Rev. and Mrs. Russell, were produced at professional stonecutters' shops in Middletown, Connecticut. But many of the early gravestones in Hadley and vicinity were local products. Dr. John Westcarre's stone, noted above, is one of several rough-hewn and crudely inscribed

Figure 28: Gravestone of John Westcarre

Figure 29: Gravestone of William Marsh

stones cut by Joseph Nash (1664-1740), a Hadley resident. Many more are known to be the work of Nathaniel Phelps and sons of Northampton, perhaps the most prolific gravestone cutters in Hampshire County during the middle decades of the eighteenth century.

Some of the earliest Phelps stones bear winged skulls and skull-like faces – grim reminders of mortality. More benign, winged faces, thought to be expressions of hope for the hereafter, became popular during the second half of the eighteenth century. The shift from winged skulls to winged faces occurred throughout southern New England, beginning around 1740. While most Hadley families patronized Joseph Nash and the Phelpses, some of the more affluent families patronized stonecutters located further afield: Thomas Johnson, William Holland, Joseph Williston, Solomon Brewer and John Ely (to name a few). Examples of these and other gravestone cutters' work are noted in the list, below.

Between 1770 and 1780, Hadley families began to patronize newly established gravestone cutters located in towns to the north and east. Gravestones in a wider range of materials and styles began to appear among the Connecticut Valley sandstones. Some families chose slate gravestones cut by John Locke and Solomon Ashley of Deerfield and by Ebenezer Janes of Northfield. Others chose stones cut from gneiss and schist at the Sikes shop in Belchertown and at one or more shops in Pelham.

By the 1790s, slate succeeded sandstone as the most common gravestone material at Old Hadley Cemetery and remained so through the 1810s. During the same time period, urns, willows and architectural motifs gained popularity and became the dominant motifs soon after 1800. Much of the impetus for these changes was provided by a few enterprising young gravestone cutters who arrived in the Connecticut Valley soon after 1800. One of the first to arrive was Alpheus Longley, a slate cutter from Shirley, Massachusetts, who settled in Hatfield in 1804. Two years later, Samuel Daugherty, another slate cutter, settled in Whately. Longley and Daugherty each placed advertisements in the

Hampshire Gazette and each signed or initialed several examples of his work. Among the early nineteenth-century gravestones at Old Hadley Cemetery are a few signed by Longley, Daugherty or Daugherty's brother-in-law, Martin Woods.

In their advertisements, Longley, Daugherty, and many of their contemporaries offered marble gravestones and monuments, as well as slate. The marble came from quarries along the western borders of Massachusetts and Vermont. In Hadley, marble succeeded slate as the principal gravestone material during the 1820s, and continued to be the most popular material through the Civil War era. The quarried blocks were cut and shaped at water-powered stone saw mills, then shipped to stonecutters and monument dealers throughout the northeastern United States. By the 1830s and 1840s, plain and simple marble forms had succeeded the more elaborately carved forms, popular during the previous century, and large family monuments had begun to appear among the rows of headstones and footstones. Hadley families could order marble monuments from a number of local stonecutters and monument dealers, including the Rankin Brothers and C.M. Kinney in Northampton—there are signed stones from both shops at Old Hadley Cemetery.

In the following list are many of the gravestone cutters whose work you will see at Old Hadley Cemetery, with one or more examples of each of their work.

Connecticut Valley Sandstone Cutters, late 17th and 18th centuries

Stanclift Shop, Middletown, Connecticut—table stones for ***Rev. John Russell*** (d. 1692) and his first wife, ***Rebekah*** (d. 1688)—these rugged sandstone monuments may be the work of James Stanclift I (1634-1712)

Joseph Nash (1664-1740), Hadley—paid for the gravestones for ***Dr. John Westcarre*** (d. 1674) in 1737; is thought to have made the granite grave post for ***Jacob Worner*** (d. 1711)

Nathaniel Phelps (1721-1789) and sons, Northampton—stones for *Sarah Porter* (d. 1775), *Deacon Jonathan Smith* (d. 1774), *Rebekkah Smith* (d. 1747)

Elijah Phelps (c.1761-1842), eldest son of Nathaniel Phelps, moved to Lanesborough, Massachusetts around 1780 and there cut gravestones from local marble—stone for Capt. *Moses Porter* (d. 1755) and his widow, **Elizabeth** (d. 1798)

Rufus Phelps (c.1766-1826), youngest son of Nathaniel Phelps, succeeded his father at the Northampton shop—stones for *Widow Sarah Eastman* (d. 1794), *Timothy Lyman* (d. 1795)

Thomas Johnson II (1718-1774), Middletown, Connecticut—stones for *Rev. Chester Williams* (d. 1753), *Hon. Eleazer Porter* (d. 1757)

Gideon Hale (1712-1776), lower Connecticut Valley—probably cut stone for *Lt. Nathaniel Alexander* (d. 1742)

William Holland (active c.1748-67), lower Connecticut Valley—stone for *Capt. Job Marsh* (d. 1746)

Joseph Williston (1732-1768), Springfield—stone for *Miriam Marsh* (d. 1765)

Solomon Brewer (1746-1824), Springfield—stone for **Sarah Hopkins** (d. 1774), wife of Rev. S. Hopkins, widow of Rev. Chester Williams, is an example of Brewer's "high style"; modeled on the work of the Johnson shop

Stebbins Shop (Ezra Stebbins, 1731-1796, et al.), Longmeadow—the stone for *Lois Porter* (d. 1792) is thought to have come from this shop [the stones for *Elizabeth Johnson* (d. 1803) and *Isaac Jonson* (d. 1808) in Hockanum are probably the work of Ezra's son, **Ebenezer Stebbins** (1773-1826) of Wilbraham]

John Ely (1735-1815), West Springfield; his second wife was Abigail (Montague) Chapin, daughter of John & Thankful

Montague of Hadley; Ely cut several stones for members of the Montague family, for example—*3 children of John and Thankful Montague* (d. 1750s); *Lt. John Montague* (d. 1803)

Swift River Valley Gneiss and Schist, late 18th century

Joseph Sikes (1743-1801) and sons, Belchertown—Joseph's wife, Eunice (Smith) was descended from the Smiths of Hadley and Hatfield—stones for *Martha Nash and her stillborn infant* (d. 1788), *Benjamin Dickinson* (d. 1778)

Pelham Stoneworks (late 18th century)—stones for *Lois Williams* (d. 1787), *Dea. Timothy Eastman* (d. 1790)

Connecticut Valley Slate Cutters, 1770s through 1840s

Ebenezer Janes (1736-1808), Northfield—stones for *Dorothy Lyman* (d. 1787), *Warham Smith* (d. 1802)

John Locke (1752-1837) and **Solomon Ashley** (1754-1823), Deerfield—matching stones for *Josiah Pierce Esq.* (d. 1788) and his widow, *Miriam* (d. 1795)

Alpheus Longley (1785-1857), Hatfield—worked in slate and marble, signed stones for *John Atwell* (d. 1805), *Oliver & Warham Smith* (d. 1806)

Samuel Daugherty (c.1778-1861), Whately and Belchertown—worked in slate and marble, signed slate stone for *Stephen Goodman* (d. 1802)

Martin Woods (1787-1859) of Belchertown and Whately, brother-in-law of Samuel Daugherty—worked in slate and marble, signed marble stone for *Robert Cook* (d. 1813); his son, **Hopkins Woods** (1813- ?) succeeded him

Samuel W. Chapin (1792-1851), Bernardston—slate stones for *Annah Chapin* (d. 1812), *Horace Judd* (d. 1831), *2 children of Horace and Joanna Judd* (d. 1827)

Rankin Brothers (Abial, 1796-1844, and Zebina 1791- ?) Pelham and Northampton, worked in slate and marble—slate stone for *Nathaniel White* (d. 1821)

Some mid-19th-century Marble Cutters

A. F. Belden Pittsfield—signed marble stone for *William Smith* (d. 1840) and his daughter, Julia (d. 1829)

Charles M. Kinney (1818-1911), Amherst and Northampton—signed marble stone for *Isabella Thompson* (d. 1844)

Moses Goodale (1797-1872), Amherst and Belchertown—listed in *The New England Business Directory*, 1860

O.M. Clapp (active, 1860), Amherst—listed in *The New England Business Directory*, 1860

Special thanks to Kevin Sweeney, Professor of History and American Studies at Amherst College, and to Fred Oakley, the guardian of Hadley cemeteries. Over the years, Kevin and I have shared the results of our research on Connecticut Valley gravestones and stonecutters. In 1999, Fred, his wife Rosalee and I transcribed and photographed the stones in the oldest (westernmost) section of Old Hadley Cemetery.

Highlights from Hadley's Town Cemeteries
Fred Oakley with Laura Miller

Fred Oakley has been conserving Hadley gravestones since 1989. His active entry into the field began at the Association for Gravestone Studies Conference held at Governor Dummer Academy in Essex County, Massachusetts, when he initiated AGS's first Conservation Workshop. He has since then led conservation workshops all across the Commonwealth, and, among other places, in New York, Illinois, Georgia, Oregon, and Washington D.C. He also contributed a conservation column to the AGS Quarterly from 1994 to 2008, covering many aspects of gravestone repair and care. Both longtime members of the Association for Gravestone Studies, Fred and his wife, Rosalee, were honored to have an award for extraordinary dedication named after them; the "Oakley Certificate of Merit" is given annually to acknowledge special contributions to the preservation and study of gravestones.

Since arriving in Hadley in 1992, Fred has been either a member or the chair of the town's Cemetery Commission. As a conservator, the first monument he treated was Reverend John Russell's table stone whose supporting pillars were failing. During the next 15 years and particularly in the four years preceding the Town's 350th Anniversary, many stones were conserved and deteriorating fences at four of the five town-owned cemeteries were replaced. He has supervised inventories of the gravestones

Figure 30: Fred Oakley in 2010

done by local students, and led numerous workshops in Hadley's cemeteries, passing his knowledge of and passion for gravestone preservation on to new generations of practitioners and conserving and repairing numerous stones along the way.

Widely known for his warmth and good humor, Fred's cemetery tours have been enjoyed by many people through the years. In the pages to follow, University of Massachusetts oral historian Laura Miller follows Fred through Hadley's five town cemeteries, capturing some of the highlights of those places—stones that Fred is particularly fond of because of the stories they tell.

When and how did you start doing this kind of work?

I retired from New England Telephone in 1986. And for the first year, I assisted the sexton at our church in Wellesley. The church had a cemetery [that was in need of much conservation work]. And so, with the rudimentary equipment I had at that time, we righted several stones. When I got involved in the Association for Gravestone Studies, I became interested in conserving old gravestones—that launched me on my way. The first conservation workshop we had was in 1989 in Essex County and after that, every year at the AGS annual conference, I developed a scheme called "learn by doing." The idea is that you do the work and see that cleaning a stone is a very simple task, but resetting a stone or casting a stone is demanding in terms of use of equipment and materials. And I also connected with Greenfield Community College and held workshops in Hadley.

I'm trying to preserve the history in these town cemeteries and this is where the town's history is. It's all right here.

How do the stones relate to the orientation of graves?

During the colonial period when you read the inscription you are usually facing the east, so on the day of resurrection they would rise and face the east—essentially that was a colonial style.

Approximately how many a year do you find that you have to conserve or repair?

It's very, very difficult, because during the wintertime, the freeze-and-thaw cycle tends to make some stones lean or fall over. In the five cemeteries that we have here, I would guess right at this point, I have at least 80 stones.

How would you fix a stone that was leaning over?

I'd excavate around the stone, lift it out, and then use sand and gravel to provide a drainage bed. Then we'd set the stone in place and back fill with more sand and gravel, and then top if off with about two inches of soil sprinkled with grass seed for turf.

Now all of the repairs on the stones here, did you do them all?

No, I've only been here since 1992. When I get done with this, I don't know who is going to take over, but I've tried to train people in local towns to get them started on their cemeteries and using proper materials. Even then you find people using improper materials, like liquid nails, or Gorilla Glue! Fortunately, there are professionals who can be engaged to conserve stones should there be no one locally who has been trained in the process.

How did you learn to repair gravestones?

We have a book published by AGS called *Gravestone Preservation Primer*, and I apprenticed with people who are "professionals" in the field. From these experiences I learned methodology and where to get all of the appropriate materials to bond the stones.

Words of wisdom on cleaning gravestones:

There's no way to keep these permanently clean. Sometimes people ask me, "Mr. Oakley, if I clean this stone how long will it stay clean?" I say, "I'll tell you what to do. Take a pillow slip, wash it, hang it out on the line, wait for two years, go bring it in, and see if it's clean." I say, "That should answer your question."

It's important to keep stones clean, though. Biological growth eats the stone's surface, and it's important to keep them clean for recording purposes, too.

How did the 1936 flood affect the Old Hadley Burying Ground?

The whole cemetery was under water and in the photographs we have there were very few stones left standing.... The Civilian Conservation Corps was located close by here and they spent, according to the record, something like three months just scooping up and removing river silt and straightening and resetting the stones. You see pictures of the tri-pods—big eight-by-eight timbers with a pulley at the top—to help set the large stones. Some of the stones were not reset where the original map indicates they should be. We're told by some of the old timers that lived down in Hockanum that they found some stones in the branches of trees down there. You know, during a flood everything comes down river—animals, trees, the whole bit.

Anything else?

It's very emotionally moving.... Reading the inscriptions and epitaphs is a journey back in time for the present generation to understand and comprehend the lives of our predecessors who lived and worked and played and died in Hadley.

A Tour of the Cemeteries
with Fred Oakley
Old Hadley Cemetery

Reverend Russell and his Wife Rebekah:

In this old burying ground we have five table stones, with five legs, usually. They are essentially designed after the English style.

So this is the Reverend here, on the right hand side. And Rebekah is residing right here [on the left of Reverend Russell]....

It's interesting some of the spelling on Reverend Russell's stone. There's "c-h-e-i-f"—"Cheif Shepherd"…he died in 1692… Rebekah here died in 1688….

Rebekah Russell's stone is the oldest stone that we have extant here in the cemetery. Part of the problem of these stones was the great flood of 1936 in which this cemetery was essentially leveled, and the effort to place the stones back where they were originally, could be a little difficult because they didn't have a map, and so you find footstones mixed in with headstones in disparate sections.

It's difficult to read here but we have photographs of it. And interestingly enough, on Reverend Russell's stone you start reading along the perimeter of the gravestone and then you continue into the center.

This particular stone is a favorite of mine because when I came here, it was on the ground. So we had to crib it, jack it up on house jacks. It looks like it is thin—it is not thin at all. This rock here would weigh, oh, 1500, 1800 pounds. That why you need house jacks.

The town gave me the dollars to get four new supports made. The original supports had a bit of a shape to them but the replacement supports are simple rectangular blocks.

Margaret Hopkins

This particular motif, do you see how beautifully this is done? That's with a really fine piece of sandstone. Some of the sandstone [on other gravestones in the burying ground] is delaminating and the problem with sandstone, if it's not really good stuff, is that it wicks moisture up because it's very susceptible to water. When the water does that it begins to delaminate, and sometimes it'll just plain fall apart.

Jacob Worner [Warner]

This is known as a post stone and it is unusual not only for its unique size – about 2 ½ inches square by 18 inches high—but also for the fact that…other people look at it and say "oh, it's misspelled—Desember." I want to ask particular people that say, "oh that's a misspelling there," when was the first dictionary made available? And even when the first dictionary was made available it took awhile to get distributed [laughs].

I'm told that [post stones appear with] such infrequency that you probably would say that it's rare to find one of them. Don't bump into them at any rate…it broke and I did an adhesive repair. It's nice and sturdy now. It's Mr. Worner, Iacob Worner.

Chester Williams:

This gets to be pretty much my favorite stone. Chester Williams was a pastor and predeceased his wife, and then she remarried Hopkins and when she died there were fourteen children. The beauty, just the sheer beauty of the carving of these stones, is enough to make you fall in love with them.

These are sandstone. These are gorgeous stones and look at the handicraft, just the handicraft that went into carving these. We were told by our folks who research things that they often would put [the stones] in water, if there was a brook close by, to even soften the stone more so then it could be more easily carved. But look at the detail, and know that you don't make mistakes.

On some sandstone and slate stones, some sections are separating. Stone tends to exfoliate if moisture gets into the edges and freezes; every time moisture gets into those stones it tends to want to flake off, and then the inscription and iconography are lost. The interesting thing about these stones is they do wick moisture from the ground and that's often the reason why they disintegrate. Both sandstone and slate come from stone quarries where there are grades of stone, from poor to excellent. This stone is still in very good condition.

Chester Williams stone, detail

Isaac Chauncy

This was our second minister. This is another one of my very favorite stones. But Isaac took a direct hit—this tree right back here. And here's Isaac over here [points to crumbled remains of the original stone on the ground].

When a tree hits a stone like this, it's done for. But in this instance we happened to have a photograph of this stone, which I sent to a firm in Chicago that digitized it and made a porcelain replica. I mounted the replica to a new granite stone to replace the crushed original. That happened in 1999. Being a member of the Association for Gravestone Studies gives a person many ideas. This was one way suggested to replace a damaged historic gravestone.

Benjamin Colt

Benjamin Colt, reading in Judd's *History of Hadley*, was a Blacksmith. His great grandson founded the Colt firearms industry in Connecticut, just in time for the Civil War.

This stone has an interesting feature: originally there was an extra piece attached to the face which formed a nose. It has been lost from the headstone, but there is one in the footstone. The footstone is headed the wrong way because when the stones were reset after the 1936 flood, they weren't always set in the original place.

Chileab Smith

By far, one of my very favorite stones is this one. You see Chileab and his wife, and it is very difficult to read now, but it says "memorially they lived in marriage stat,"—marriage state—"70 years at lest." So it obviously predates the dictionary, and most of the time, I gather that the carvers who may not have been intellectually on top of things, they would go to the lawyers and the ministers who were trained in spelling. Only the top half of the stone was originally showing above the soil.

With my tripod I lifted the stone and it seemed to keep growing until the full epitaph was visible. I knew something was below the carver's groove and found a very touching sentiment. It probably weighs eight hundred pounds, there's a lot of it in the ground. But up it came, and all of this became visible for us to share and to enjoy.

Major John Smith

Since my great-great grandfather served during the American Revolution, this became sort of a special stone for me. This gentleman was a major in the Army of the Revolution, and on the east side is his first wife, on the north side is his second wife, and on the west is his third wife. Though we have no specific record of the cause of deaths of his several wives, it is likely that disease of childbirth problems took them. In those days when your wife died, you sought another mate immediately to care for the children. Likewise when the husband predeceased the wife, she needed to find another mate to provide for the household.

Ishmael Prutt

The Prutts were an African American family who were slaves here in Hadley. Ishmael was born in slavery, but slavery was outlawed after Massachusetts wrote its first state constitution, so he was a free man when he died, but most freed slaves lived in poverty, so this stone was probably purchased by his former owners. Ishmael's death date was June 26, 1809, at age of 83, the earliest known African American burial here in our cemetery.

John Morison

His name is John Morison, his death date was September 13th, 1814. He was about 65 years old. He was a Scotch Highlander. He was captured with Colonel Campbell in Boston Harbor on June 1776 and he "died in the family of Charles Phelps, September 13th, 1814. " Apparently, when the Revolutionary War concluded, he chose to remain, found a job at the Charles Phelps farm, and never returned home.

The Children of Mr. Mathew & Mrs. Sarah Cadwell

I thought this one was particularly interesting…. The children of Mr. Mathew and Mrs. Sarah Cadwell. Sarah died on the 1st of March [1803] at the age of twelve weeks; she was the namesake of her mother. And then Orange—an unusual name—died the 13th of February 1805 at the age of one. Then Rufus died 5th of May 1807, [at the age of] eleven days. So when you look back over that period of time, from 1803 to 1807, you wonder if there was some kind of disease being spread in town, or if a genetic flaw caused these children to die so quickly. But it's always so sad to read about this. Nowadays, [modern medicine] might have saved these children, but the medicine back at the turn of the nineteenth century was not terribly advanced in comparison to what we have today.

You see this particular stone was probably placed here after the third child died. The stone clearly is hand carved, so you don't have a hand carver to come out here and carve an upright stone. Nowadays with the granites and what have you, if you need to add a date or something of this nature, a person comes out with a truck, with all of his equipment on, and puts a mask on, and it's done. This is all done by hand. It would be done at one time. And there's an urn and willow, and that became very popular—if you see a stone [with this motif] you can almost bet the house 1797 would be the first time they would show up and then all through the early 1800s…the willow symbolizes sorrow, and the urn is a repository of the mortal remains…. In a number of instances you see stones that were placed probably many years after the death of the person.

North Hadley Cemetery

George Henry

I found this stone very interesting because of the symbolism on the gravestone. Can you guess what it is? It's a grand piano. He was the son of Nathan & Polly W. Clark, and his date of death and what have you is on there and this symbol indicates that this lad was a musician. He was 19 years old when he passed away. This right down here [at the bottom of the stone] is called an epitaph and often you see this in upper and lower case, very well done. When they carved this particular piece down there they made it so small that it's very difficult to read, so what we do is clean the stone first and then, on a day like this, it catches the sunlight and you can see and read the stone. Then there are books that we have that will say, "oh, this was a poem," and "this was a line from a poem." Sometimes it would just have a biblical verse like John 3:16 or Psalm 21 or something of this nature, and other times the epitaph is a brief statement, like "gone to heaven."

The Smith Family

You see this hill up here? That clearly indicates that it was built up; there was more soil brought in. And when you see the two monuments up here, you can understand that there was, shall we say, some wealth involved…its particular elevation above the rest indicates great wealth. There's an interesting inscription on this side: Caleb, a Captain—he was probably a sea captain—died in Melbourne, Australia. That's a long way away. And Mary, his wife, died a year earlier; she was 33, he was 35. I'm wondering if he brought something contagious back with him. And then Henry Smith died soon after returning from Australia, 1854. He was aged 26…. But this whole inscription is interesting to read.

On the opposite side of the monument the part that I want to read is "Thomas Gerry at the age of 55 and Alice Smith, his wife"—notice it's her maiden name—"age 46 both instantly

killed in auto at Hadley railroad crossing, April 11, 1910." And what I found interesting about this…is in 1910, how many people owned automobiles? Do you know where the bike path goes underneath Route 9? That's where the crossing was. And how they ran into a train or a train ran into them, I don't know, but apparently there were no warning gates.

The burial sites are presumably under the many smaller stones surrounding the monument. If you look over here, the stone border surrounding the family plot is called curbing. And the gentleman over there, Mr. Granger [pointing out another obelisk on the opposite side of the cemetery] decided that he didn't want to be in competition for size, so he chose a lot on the far side of the cemetery. These two lots, the Smith and Granger lots, are the only two burial sites raised above the general level of the cemetery and the only two that have curbing.

Frederick S. Russell

I come from the South, born and reared. I was born in North Carolina and reared in Georgia. And you see something like this, the Battle of Chantilly, it was early on in the "War of Northern Aggression" [laughs]...but identifying where he perished in that particular battle, it's really quite interesting. You can often find information about where these people are interred. We do have two young men down there who were working in Hadley, one was a farmer and the other worked in a wire factory. One of them died of disease in Washington, D.C. but it doesn't say where he was interred. And the other one just sort of disappeared. My effort has been to try to locate where the interment might have been after battles.

It's likely that he [Frederick Russell] is interred here because during the Civil War if there was something to transport, they often put them in lead-lined coffins and shipped them back home.

We replace every flag every year, because during the winter they become tattered. And as you notice here [on the flag holder], it says G.A.R., Grand Army of the Republic. The flag holder was probably placed there shortly after the Civil War...it's cast iron, and now we're using bronze, and we use the generic bronze now so that you don't have to separate from the French and Indian War, the Revolutionary War...now they just say "Veteran."

Mr. Benjamin Smith

I found this stone interesting because it's in memory of Mr. Benjamin Smith. He was found dead in the Connecticut River, 10 September 1801, at the age of 66. And the river still takes people. Found dead in the Connecticut River...it's interesting he was found in the Connecticut River, which means it was just over there a piece, and so rather than being done in Northampton or in the Meadows [he was interred here]...this person lived in Northampton, and it didn't say exactly where in the Connecticut River, but I find it interesting because he was found dead, as the inscription says.

They [the gravestones] speak to me in these kinds of terms; they're part of the history of this little sub-community here. Hadley was five different little communities, and reading the stones and seeing how they've expressed the presence of this person often I find very interesting historically. Every time I conserve a gravestone I usually talk to the person. Like if I was getting ready to clean Henriette there [points to another stone], I'd say "Henriette, we're getting ready to clean your stone because you're sort of messy." [laughing].... When people start to clean a stone, you're just not cleaning a stone, you're cleaning a stone for a person, or a family, and that adds to the importance and maybe the satisfaction.

Russellville Cemetery

John Russell

When you walk in [to the cemetery] it's Russell, Russell, Russell, Russell, all over the place.... In this particular cemetery, the Russells make up roughly twenty-five percent. Many of these pieces of land were given by somebody for a cemetery, or if you will, in Old Hadley we call it a burying ground. So this probably was once a farm field. Just like Old Hadley was farm field.

Here's John. The symbolism is a furled flag and a musket meaning the war is over. But notice when he was killed: member of Company D, 27th Massachusetts Volunteers, killed in the Battle at Cold Harbor, June 30, 1864, aged 24 years. If you read anything about the Battle of Cold Harbor…it was horrible. And notice here at the bottom, only son of John and Persis Russell. And this would be dad and his son, they're both here.

A furled flag over a musket [is one symbol found on Civil War gravestones], and oftentimes you'll find on the stones cannons with the barrel turned down, meaning it's the end [of the Civil War].

Carrie E. and Dexter B. Wiley

I selected this particular stone [Carrie E. Wiley] because of the symbolism. It's a lily of the valley, and oftentimes you find on stones the furled flag over the musket, or a cannon with its barrel headed down, and when we get down to Hockanum there's [a stone with] a thistle, which would be a symbol of a Scot. So I want you to get an idea—see this is a lily of the valley also associated there [on Dexter B. Wiley's stone]. That's the kind of symbolism that often is very appealing to people.

But when you go to clean this stone, cleaning all the little detail is extremely difficult. We're often told to use a toothbrush, but the chances of getting it bright and sparkly are from zero to none, because it's too finely carved and you don't want to get in there and start messing around and break any of these things. This is a husband and wife. [The intricate carvings] probably took a lot of effort, but see they're not hand-carved. They're machine carved; when I say machine carved I mean using a power unit…so that's how all of this was done. You don't find these [kinds of stones] hand-carved—slate is hand-carved.

Mary C. Wiley

This is Mary Wiley, 1845 to 1919. Sort of undistinguished, right? But this [points to the flag holder] is what makes it very distinguished. Woman's Relief Corps, Massachusetts Department, Corps 116. Guess what? It's alive and well today...It was founded to give support to the Union soldiers and subsequently over a period of time they broadened it to all soldiers. But you never hear anything about it, except this little flag holder. By rights, you see, she would not be considered a veteran. I've only seen two of these in Hadley, there might be more. But that was what caught my attention, and the history behind it. And [in 1962] Congress passed an act endorsing the Woman's Relief Corps.

This is not the only group that has specific flag holder markers, there are firemen, there are police, there are others, like Woodmen of the World—ever heard of the Woodmen of the World? Interestingly enough, if you had an insurance policy with Woodmen of the World—it's an insurance company. And part of the value of belonging to that was that they provided you with a gravestone.

About three or four years ago I called Jones Library and she said, "yes, here's the information." And today, I looked on the website and there it is—Woman's Relief Corps.

Plainville Cemetery

Edward Howard, his wife Hulda J., and their three sons: Charles C., Daniel S., and Henry E.

This is a stone that appealed to me.... All three of their sons were buried "at the South"—it says "at the South" rather than "in the South." There are three boys right here, Henry, Daniel and Charlie, all three passed away during the [Civil] war. The casualty rate was substantial, shall we say.

In North Hadley there must be 15 or 16 veterans [buried in the cemetery], not that they were all casualties [of the Civil War]. But this I thought was particularly moving because all of their boys are here—two of them in 1861, one in August, one in April, and the other in 1862.... "Their sons buried at the South"—it's very painful.

Taylor family

This is one of the more unique monuments. It's called a white bronze—except it's not bronze. It's mostly zinc. And one of the values of this particular type of material, which went out of fashion fairly quickly, was when you had a death you'd just call them and they'd send you another panel. You'd take this panel off, send it, and they'd send you a new panel [indicates the panels on all four sides]. I think in Hadley this is the only white bronze—in Hadley none of the cemeteries have any Victorian monumental art like grieving angels. Mostly you'll find that particular material will be in the Catholic cemeteries. All of our cemeteries are non-denominational.

It's hollow. And did you notice any moss or lichens on it? It's not edible! [laughs] [One of our members] researched this and actually the original castings were made down in Connecticut and then they outsourced them to other places. As a matter of fact, I found two of them in Des Moines, Iowa. And these [next to the monument] are little footstones. You'll find a lot of Civil War monuments with the soldiers up top made of white bronze. [The name "white bonze"] sold better than zinc: zinc was used for tubs and washboards.

Hockanum Cemetery

About the stone wall at the cemetery:

An early feature of this particular cemetery is that this wall here—down to the break right there—was done by the WPA [Works Progress Administration] and therefore, it has become what our Historical Commission calls "historically significant." And what people don't really understand, which I know—see there was an opening down there? And see something popping up from the edge? This cemetery wall extends almost to the South Hadley sign. But it's below grade, because during the wintertime, when they come along and plow, that's where all this stuff comes from, sand and gravel....

This part here [the newer portion of the stone wall] was done in 1957 when Stuart Russell donated this part of his farmland in return for a burying site.

Irving McClure Johnson and Electa Search Johnson

This is Irving and Exy. "Home is the sailor home from the sea." Irving McClure Johnson, Captain U.S. Naval Reserves, July 4, 1905 to January 1991, and his wife and shipmate Electa—we always called her "Exy"—Search Johnson. That was her middle name; it's unusual. August 17, 1909. Now her death date has not been inscribed on here yet, but this is the Brigantine [the ship pictured on the gravestone] and people would buy into pieces of the trip and Exy was "chief cook and bottle washer." She did the whole bit. Two issues of National Geographic over a period of time followed the Brigantine and I once mentioned to Exy that my family—part of my family—who were Huguenots, left from a harbor down in Southwestern France, she said "oh, that's a beautiful harbor!" [They went to] Indonesia, all over the world, and they made friends everyplace they went. So when her body was cremated we had the service at the church, and a number of people took parts of the remains and took them back to their home countries too.

I saw a video of her [Exy] and here she was climbing the mast, and I looked over and I said, "Exy, what in God's name were you doing up there?" And she said, "Setting the sails, that's what you have to do on ships like this!"

Roger Johnson

Now this is Roger…he died in 1988, [and his wife] Elsie. 1918 the Johnson's Bookstore [opened, and was running until] 1978, that's a good period of time, that's sixty years. "They kept an open door and a warm welcome for all who crossed their path." Isn't that lovely? And these [images carved on the top] are indications, this is a Morgan horse, this is a Knox—it's a car—and this is an antique bicycle.

It's slate. These are quality slates. As I told you there's the good, better, and the very best, and so with Johnson we have the very best.

Ebenezer Pomeroy

[The sandstone marker] back over here…there was a PeeGee Hydrangea; it had grown up right behind it, and the top had broken off and the hydrangea, as it grew, grew over the top part of it. So the question was, how could I get it in the kind of shape so that I could remove the tree from the stone without damaging the stone.

With careful use of a chain saw I removed the offending tree trunk, removed the stone and competed removing the hydrangea stump. It took an hour and ten minutes for me to release the stump. It was so large I couldn't roll it out of the excavation. The town highway department took care of it, after which I reset the stone in its original place and bonded the upper part to the lower part.

Endnotes

1 Kevin M. Sweeney, "Gravestones," in William Hosley, ed., *The Great River: Art and Society of the Connecticut River* (Hartford: Wadsworth Atheneum, 1985), 485.

2 Sara Chase, et al, *Preservation Guidelines for Municipally Owned Historic Burial Grounds and Cemeteries, 2nd edition* (MA Dept of Environmental Management, June 2002), 5. This essay relies heavily on Chase's invaluable work, as well as Sweeney's essential study, "Gravestones."

3 Though gravestones were not necessarily erected in the same year as the death they marked, for simplicity's sake this essay will describe the stones by that date.

4 See Laurel Thatcher Ulrich, "Hannah Barnard's Cupboard," in Marla R. Miller, ed., *Cultivating a Past: Essays on the History of Hadley, Massachusetts* (Amherst: University of Massachusetts Press, 2009), 154-190.

5 Sweeney, "Gravestones,"486.

6 James Deetz, *In Small Things Forgotten* (New York: Anchor, 1996).

7 Chase, et al, *Preservation Guidelines*, 6.

8 The committee included Seth Smith, Eleazer Porter Esq., Oliver Smith, Nathaniel White, and Samuel Gaylord.

9 This committee included Lt. Elijah Smith, Maj. Sylvester Smith, and Jason Stockbridge.

10 Members were the Rev. Dan Huntington, Hon. Samuel Porter, and Sereno Smith.

11 Town assessor Elisha Dickinson, selectman Oliver Bonney, and town clerk and treasurer Giles C. Kellog served this time.

12 Hampshire County Registry of Deeds Book 399, pg. 445; Cemetery Committee Report, 1887.

13 These paragraphs draw particularly heavily on Chase, et al, *Preservation Guidelines,* 6-10.

14 Chase, et al, *Preservation Guidelines,* 9.

15 The committee men included J.B. Porter, L.N. Granger, Horace Russell, Daniel Cowles, and Elijah H. Bartlett. This original Cemetery Committee was reorganized in 1872.

16 In the report for the year ending 1 March, 1877, $9.15 is recorded as paid to Dr. Franklin Bonney for trees for the cemeteries.

17 In 1897, the hearse house at North Hadley was moved, although the 16 February 1898 Cemetery Committee report does not specify where from or to. The location of the second hearse house is unknown, but it was most likely at Center Cemetery as the 1887 Cemetery Committee report references painting the Center hearse.

18 Cemetery Committee Report, 1970. At the time of this report two of these roadways were divided into burial lots.

19 Cemetery Committee Report, 1890.

20 Cemetery Committee Report, 1895.

21 The fence on the north side collapsed in 1932, and was replaced with 50 rod fencing and posts in 1933. Cemetery Committee Report, 1932.

22 Cemetery Committee Report, 1893.

23 Cemetery Committee Report, 1896.

24 Cemetery Committee Report, 1899.

25 "Holy Rosary Cemetery," clipping in the collections of the Hadley Historical Society. Our thanks to Peg Miller for supplying this information.

26 Hampshire County Registry of Deeds, Book 627, pg. 295.

27 In 1912 the pump was connected to the town water supply, supplanting the well system previously used. In 1913 the committee took on the large task of erecting both a steel-covered storage house (a cement floor added in 1934), and new fencing.

28 Mass General Laws Chapter 280, April 1911.

29 Cemetery Committee Report, 1937.

30 *The Springfield Republican*, 1 January 1933.

31 For the Hockanum cemetery; see http://www.hampshirecountyhistory.com/hadley/hk/index.html.

32 Cemetery Committee Report, 1932.

33 Cemetery Committee Reports, 1934, 1935.

34 The 1930s proved to be a time of dramatic change for the landscape of Hockanum Cemetery. In 1934 Samuel M. Russell gifted land 8 ft. in width at the north end of the cemetery, allowing the committee to move the fence 8 ft. to the north, and providing room for a driveway at the rear of the cemetery.

35 Hadley Tercentenary Report in Annual Town Report, 1959.

36 Cemetery Committee Report, 1938.

37 Cemetery Committee Reports, 1955, 1957.

38 Cemetery Committee Reports, 1954, 1955, 1956.

39 Cemetery Committee Report, 1957.

40 Cemetery Committee Report, 1969.

41 Cemetery Committee Report, 1962. As of this writing, no information is available as to whether those rubbings are available today.

42 Cemetery Committee Report, 1968.

43 Cemetery Committee Report, 1964.
44 Penny Humphrey, "Years blur history on Hadley," undated clipping, Dorothy Russell Papers, Hadley Historical Society; and "timeline of events for historical room," Dorothy M. Russell, ibid.
45 The nominations to the National Register for Historic Places can be accessed at Goodwin Memorial Library.
46 Report of Hadley Historical Commission, 1999. Also, after coexisting with the town Cemetery Committee for about 112 years, the North Hadley Cemetery Association voted to disband in late December 2004.
47 Cemetery Committee Report, 2003.
48 The Hadley Historical Society provided funding for software and for processing the digital photographs of each stone. The project was completed 24 September 2003; copies were placed in the Town Clerk's Office and with the Historical Commission.
49 Cemetery Committee Reports, 2003, 2004.
50 Cemetery Committee Report, 2005.
51 Reports of Hadley Historical Commission, 2001, 2002.
52 Cemetery Committee Reports, 2003, 2004, 2006.
53 The completed outline for the improvement of the cemeteries for the anniversary appears in the Cemetery Committee report in 2006.
54 *Daily Hampshire Gazette,* 3 March 1997.
55 Kevin M. Sweeney, "Gravestones," 485.

www.ingramcontent.com/pod-product-compliance
Lightning Source LLC
Chambersburg PA
CBHW031200090426
42736CB00009B/749